MAQS

MUSEUM

of the

AMERICAN

QUILTER'S

SOCIETY

Additional copies of this book may be ordered from:

American Quilter's Society
P.O. Box 3290
Paducah, KY 42002-3290

@$9.95. Add $1.00 for postage & handling.

Copyright: American Quilter's Society, 1995

QUILTS

The Permanent Collection – MAQS, Vol. II

Quilts purchased/acquired

during the years

1991 through 1994

American Quilter's Society

P. O. Box 3290 • Paducah, KY 42002-3290

INTRODUCTION

In the early 1980's Bill and Meredith Schroeder were introduced to the world of quilts, and by 1984 they had begun to build an organization dedicated to promoting the accomplishments of today's quilters – the American Quilter's Society (AQS), with thousands of members worldwide. The Schroeders quickly realized the need for a collection of the quilts being produced by today's quiltmakers, and thus began the Schroeder Collection.

From 1984 through 1990, a total of 91 quilts were purchased, acquired through Purchase Awards, or received by donations. In April 1991, a catalog of that collection was published – *Quilts: The Permanent Collection – MAQS*. These quilts were also displayed to the public in the newly opened Museum of the American Quilter's Society (MAQS), a 30,000 square foot facility in Paducah, KY, which was designed and constructed especially for the display of quilts and the housing of this collection. Dedicated to honoring today's quiltmaker, this non-profit museum continues to share with visitors selections from this permanent collection.

Since 1991, many more quilts have been added to the collection, and have been shown regularly at MAQS. Because the collection has grown and changing exhibits of other contemporary quilts and antique quilts are displayed in two of the museum's three galleries, only a selection of quilts from the collection can be on display at any given time. To enable quilt lovers to enjoy all of the fine quilts added to the collection after publication of the first catalog, MAQS and AQS are proud to present this new publication, a second volume which features a full-color photograph of each of the quilts added to the permanent collection, along with comments from the maker and his or her photograph.

Though a range of work by today's quiltmakers is now represented in the MAQS Collection, development of the collection continues to be ongoing. The current MAQS Collection and this publication are offered as a second chapter in the museum's ongoing documentation of today's quiltmaking. The Schroeders and the Museum of the American Quilter's Society look forward to additions to the collection and to future volumes sharing this growing account of work by today's quiltmakers.

AIR SHOW (#153)

Jonathan Shannon

I have always loved early airplanes from a design standpoint, as well as for their emotional and romantic images. They were a natural subject for a quilt. Continuing my exploration of time and space begun in my sunflower quilt "July," I set about to create with fabric a sense of air and the weight of air that holds up airplanes. The smaller planes are set within an atmosphere of time, yet are all part of the same space. As the first male winner of the AQS Best of Show Award, I hope that this win will encourage other men to enter the quilt world and demonstrate to them how welcome they will be as quiltmakers.

AIR SHOW, 81" x 81",
Jonathan Shannon,
Belvedere, California, ©1992;
cotton; machine pieced
and hand quilted;
Best of Show Award,
1993 AQS Show.

ALETSCH (#100)

"Aletsch" is part of a series of quilts that represent my efforts to synthesize my sensory responses to a particular space: the vast mountainous basin in the Swiss Alps that encloses the Aletsch Glacier, the largest in Europe. In the summer of 1988 I spent several days hiking along its perimeter, which extends many kilometers down from the Jungfrau firn. What impressed me most was the very audible sound of millions of gallons of water rushing unseen beneath the perfectly still expanse of glacier. It seemed incongruous: the unrelenting movement of so much water and the stony rigidity of so much ice. Combined with the brilliance of the light and the clarity of the air, that incongruity made for a very memorable scenario.

Michael James

ALETSCH, 83" x 41", Michael James,
Somerset Village, Massachusetts;
1990; machine pieced and machine
quilted.

AMISH EASTER BASKETS (#118)

Elsie Vredenburg

I have sewed since I was 13, making most of my own, and later my family's clothes. My grandmother got me started quilting when I was about 17, but I had always slept under quilts and have always been fascinated by them. Even today, a blanket just doesn't "feel right." Even so, I often wondered, "Why quilting?" I still can't answer that question in so many words, but a few years ago we were watching a TV interview with a singer. When the interviewer asked her if making a comeback was worth the uphill struggle, she answered "I can't NOT sing." I turned to my husband and said, "That's it! I can't NOT quilt." It's a part of who I am.

AMISH EASTER BASKETS,
86" x 110", Elsie Vredenburg, Tustin,
Michigan, 1987; cottons;
machine pieced and hand quilted;
Third Place Award,
Theme (Baskets), 1988 AQS Show.

ANCIENT DIRECTIONS (#99)

Alison Goss

Coming from an academic background that involved no formal art training but lots of home sewing, I saw quiltmaking as a very enjoyable and exciting craft. However, over time I have found it necessary to learn more and more about artistic principles, in order to express important ideas and feelings. Inspiration from Pueblo Indian pottery and a strong appreciation for the Native American way of life led to the creation of this quilt. The central image was drafted in mirror-image perspective, and each small section was machine pieced to paper, using a method I have developed to ensure all the pieces fit together accurately.

ANCIENT DIRECTIONS, 80" x 67",
Alison Goss, Hockessin, Delaware,
1991; cottons; machine pieced and
machine quilted; Best Wall Quilt Award,
1991 AQS Show.

BASKETS AND THE CORN (#132)

Jan Lanahan

Baskets, especially corn baskets, were so important to early man that the Native Americans raised this utilitarian object to an art form. This quilt is an original design that evolved after finishing another quilt in which I used Seminole patchwork in rows to represent layers of earth. It hit me that I could "build" Native American basket designs using this technique. I used natural fiber fabrics to make row after row of tiny Seminole patchwork and added a group of coiled baskets in the center, hand painted with dyes. The brown background is the red soil of the Southwest.

BASKETS AND THE CORN,
67" x 80", Jan Lanahan, Walkersville,
Maryland, 1986; cottons and linens;
embroidered, hand painted,
machine pieced, and hand quilted;
First Place Award, Theme (Baskets),
1988 AQS Show.

BEACH ROSES (#102)

This quilt was inspired by the low, rambling roses that grow along the seashore. Both white and pink blooms often appear to grow on the same bush as a result of their ever entwining vines. The quilt is made in what is now regarded as my no-block style of quiltmaking. There is one block in the lower right of the quilt, but though the same flower repeats, the block shape disappears. This happened unconsciously as I created the quilt and was quite a pleasant surprise. I was pleased to discover that I did not need to be locked into a block shape. I could forever be free of it, able to develop beyond it if I chose.

Joyce Murrin

BEACH ROSES, 79" x 49", Joyce Murrin, Orient, New York, 1986; cotton, cotton blends, and polyester fabrics (some hand-dyed); machine pieced and hand quilted.

BOAT IN A BOTTLE SAMPLER (#135)

Lyn Peare Sandberg

I believe individual innovation has been the hallmark of women's quilt art throughout its history and I have strived to preserve this in my contemporary work. In turn, this effort has perpetuated my own artistic motivation, integrity, and style. Each bottle in this quilt contains a particular moment in a decade of sailing on the Monterey Bay, with the feathery nautilus quilting serving as a sustaining wind moving through the quilt. My husband is a boatbuilder and model maker at heart. Making this quilt relieved my sailing energy when my husband dry docked our dinghy for the season.

BOAT IN A BOTTLE SAMPLER,
80" x 92", Lyn Peare Sandberg,
Capitola, California, ©1989; cottons;
machine pieced and hand quilted;
Third Place Award, Innovative
Pieced, Professional,
1989 AQS Show.

BROWN COUNTY LOG CABINS (#129)

$\mathbf{M}$y treatment of this traditional pattern was influenced by the area in which I live. Brown County, Indiana, is heavily wooded, the hilly countryside dotted by little log cabins. This beautiful place has been home to many artists since the early part of this century. The geometric quality of the blocks and lattice strips is softened by the wavy lines of the quilting. The border quilting echoes the little "mountains" and rolling hills of Brown County, and the edging of "pine-tree points" (a variation on Prairie Points I worked out) represents the deep green woods that surround us here.

Linda Karel Sage

BROWN COUNTY LOG CABINS,
82" x 98", Linda Karel Sage,
Morgantown, Indiana, 1985; cottons
and blends; machine pieced and
hand quilted; First Place Award,
Traditional Pieced, Amateur,
1986 AQS Show.

CELEBRATION (#138)

Joyce W. Stewart

I have been quilting for about 14 years. At first I was going to make this quilt as a New Year's Eve quilt and then I decided that it could go along with any kind of celebration – birthday, anniversary, new job, new house, etc. – therefore the name "Celebration." The lines in the quilt were part of a wild material I bought, which I combined with solid colors, most of which I hand dyed myself, to get the range I wanted. I have a great love for quilting and everything that goes along with it.

CELEBRATION, 47" x 47", Joyce W. Stewart, Rexburg, Idaho, 1988; cottons; machine pieced, hand quilted, embellished with rhinestones; Honorable Mention Award, 1988 AQS Show.

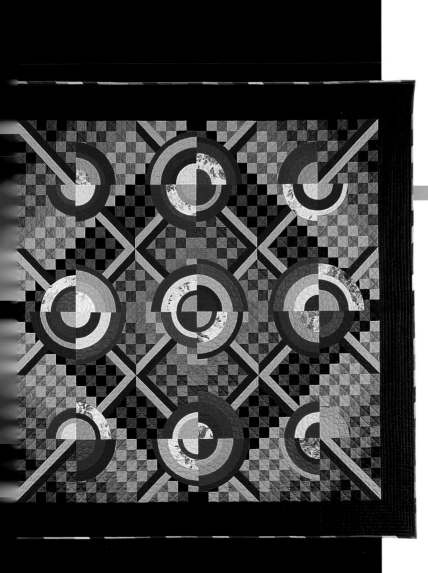

CELEBRATION OF AUTUMN (#139)

I began sewing before high school, and my original major at the University of Utah was in the field of home economics, though I finished with a degree in sociology. My first quilting class was in 1976 after I retired from my job as a social worker. I continue to take classes and enjoy participating in the world of quilting. A floral centerpiece at a reception for a special California quiltmaker was the inspiration for this quilt. The party was fun and doing the quilt was a most enjoyable challenge.

Karmen Streng

CELEBRATION OF AUTUMN,
86" x 86", Karmen Streng, Davis,
California, 1985; cottons; machine
pieced and hand quilted; Second
Place Award, Innovative Pieced,
Amateur, 1986 AQS Show.

CHERRY ROSE (#115)

Margie T. Karavitis

This quilt was inspired by a trip to the grocery store. I can never pass the magazine racks without checking all the quilt books. In one I found an antique Cherry Rose quilt being used as a background for a display of antiques and was ready to being a new project. I used cardboard templates to make circles, which I appliquéd from the back. I used an extra-loft batting and quilted around each appliquéd piece, which gives it a padded appearance. The quilt in the photograph did not show a border, but I added one and echo-quilted around the vines and cherry clusters.

CHERRY ROSE, 96" x 96", Margie T. Karavitis, Spokane, Washington, 1989; cotton; hand appliquéd, hand and machine pieced, and hand quilted.

CHIPS AND WHETSTONES (#116)

Through quiltmaking, I have come to know Mississippi in a very special way – through its people. Quilting has caused me to travel to many places and meet many people. As a former librarian, the historical side of quilting is appealing to me. I've read and thought about the connection of quilting to women's lives. In this society of fragmented time, I see my quiltmaking as a reinforcement of the family value of passing on the tradition from one generation to another. Because I used fabrics accumulated from years of sewing for my children and various home-related projects, "Chips and Whetstones" has the overall look of an old quilt. I could not have gotten that look from new fabrics I purchased.

Martha B. Skelton

CHIPS AND WHETSTONES, 79" x 89",
Martha B. Skelton, Vicksburg, Mississippi,
1987; cottons; hand and machine pieced,
hand appliquéd, and hand quilted;
Traditional Pieced, Professional,
1988 AQS Show.

CONWAY ALBUM
(I'M NOT FROM BALTIMORE) (#164)

Irma Gail Hatcher

This quilt took a year to make, but I wrote a book on how to make it at the same time. First I made the small blocks, then the center and outside blocks. Flowers from the small blocks were used in the center block and borders, adding continuity to the whole quilt. The only real decision I had to make in the design was whether to add the little triangles around the appliquéd blocks. Now I think they are one of the best ideas in the whole quilt. Making the quilt gave me great pleasure, and now I have the pleasure of knowing that it will be cared for at MAQS.

CONWAY ALBUM (I'M NOT FROM BALTIMORE), 86" x 89", Irma Gail Hatcher, Conway, Arkansas, 1992; cottons; hand appliquéd and hand quilted; Gingher Award for Hand Workmanship, 1994 AQS Show.

CORN CRIB (#112)

Adabelle Dremann

After many years of teaching art, in 1985 I started to make original pictorial quilts, and had to learn the art of appliqué to accomplish this. My first quilt, in Amateur Appliqué, was hung in the 1986 AQS Show; the second in 1987. Neither placed in the judging. I was thrilled just to be there, and learned each time from the critiques and by just looking. In 1990 I made a first wall quilt, hoping to finish it in one year. "Corn Crib" used sketches (from an old sketch book) of a crib on our farm, sketches used for a painting 25 years before. Making it in cloth was a labor of love that brought me great joy. I was always fascinated by the shape of farm wagons in the corn crib driveway, when the doors were open with the sun shining – as could be seen from my kitchen door.

–December 1991

CORN CRIB, 42" x 47", Adabelle Dremann (1910–1992), Princeton, Illinois, 1989; cottons; machine pieced, hand appliquéd, and hand quilted; First Place Award, Pictorial Wall Quilt, 1990 AQS Show.

COUNTRY SCHOOL (#114)

Adabelle Dremann

I made my first quilt in 1934, and also made a baby crib quilt of nursery rhyme characters that year. Fifty years passed before I again made quilts – five of them. All have been original appliqué and all have hung in American Quilter Society shows. In the 1989 show, this quilt won a second place award. Thoughts of a one-room country school, in a time now gone, are near to my heart. My children started to school in such a place, near our farm home in Bureau County, Illinois. The years grow shorter now, but are full of many rewarding memories, and hopefully a few more quilts.

–December 1991

COUNTRY SCHOOL, 73" x 92",
Adabelle Dremann (1910–1992),
Princeton, Illinois, 1988; cottons;
machine pieced, hand appliquéd,
and hand quilted; Second Place,
Appliqué, Amateur, 1989 AQS Show.

DAWN SPLENDOR (#106)

Nancy Ann Sobel

The inspiration for this quilt came from early morning bird watching with my son, viewing the soft grayed colors and noticing the silvery spider webs in the grass and corners of the porch. When looking for just the right color for the peony blossoms, I found a perfect piece of tie-dyed fabric my daughter had made. However, another tie-dyeing project led to an unplanned addition. My daughter had used the clothes dryer to complete that tie-dyeing process. I prewashed the nine yards of muslin for the backing and after drying it, found several little spots of color left from the tie-dyeing project! I decided that the peony ants on the front could crawl to the back of the quilt, too. Several were inked on the back to cover the spots. We observed that robins were the first to sing at dawn, so I quilted robins in the large star points.

DAWN SPLENDOR, 94" x 94", Nancy Ann
Sobel, Brooktondale, New York, 1991;
cottons; machine pieced, hand
appliquéd, and hand quilted;
Best of Show Award, 1991 AQS Show.

DESCENDING VISIONS (#141)

Dawn Amos

I have entered the AQS show every year since 1987, and was delighted to win a second Best Wall Quilt award. From early on, my goal has been to be able to make a living with my quiltmaking. This goal was furthered in 1992 by an Emergining Arts Grant from the state of South Dakota. When designing a quilt, the first thing I do is draw the image full size. Using reverse appliqué and freezer paper appliqué, I then create the pictorial quilt. I dye most of the fabric in my quilts, using self-taught dyeing skills.

DESCENDING VISIONS, 46" x 62",
Dawn Amos, Rapid City, South
Dakota, 1992; hand-dyed cottons;
hand appliquéd and hand quilted;
Best Wall Quilt Award,
1992 AQS Show.

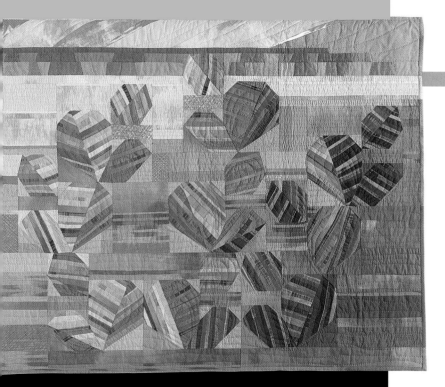

DESERT DUSK (#150)

Marguerite Ann Malwitz

For many years I was a weaver whose primary concern was the execution of large pictorial tapestry commissions. This without a doubt has influenced my work as I made a gradual change over to quiltmaking. Presently my quilts are inspired by the American landscape. My direction is to translate scenic vistas into simple designs and to concentrate on the creative selection and use of fabrics. I am also fascinated by texture, surface design, and embellishment, all of which are important to my work. "Desert Dusk" was inspired by the simple lines and complex color changes in the Arizona desert and also by a visit to the Desert Botanical Gardens in Phoenix.

DESERT DUSK, 53" x 43", Marguerite
Ann Malwitz, Brookfield, Connecticut,
1988; cottons, blends, silks, and satin;
tie-dyed, machine and hand pieced,
hand quilted; First Place Award,
Wall Quilt, Amateur, 1988 AQS Show.

DIFFRACTIONS III (#131)

Mary Morgan

"Diffractions II" was the third in a series I began in 1984 in a Nancy Crow workshop. It includes many hand-dyed gradations arranged to give a feeling of depth. Color is my primary interest. I use hand-dyed and overdyed fabrics to give me the color fields that are the most important elements. Pattern and form are secondary, usually limited to one or two simple repeated shapes. I come from a background of making traditional quilts and have a deep respect for the generations of quiltmakers who created works of beauty without the benefit of formal art training or abundant materials. I'm concerned with what my quilts do, not so much with what they say. Working with color gives me joy. If I can share that joy with the viewer for a moment, then I am content.

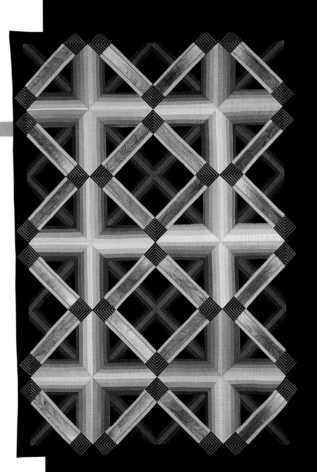

DIFFRACTIONS III, 65" x 94", Mary Morgan, Little Rock, Arkansas, 1989; cottons, commercial and hand dyed; machine pieced and hand quilted.

DISCOVERY (#160)

Francelise Dawkins

I invented the word "silkollage" to describe my intricate fabric artwork, in which four layers of material are quilted, appliquéd, embroidered, or painted on. Fascinated by the variety and quality of fiberworks in the United States, I studied quilting, printing, and piecing techniques, to give my collages added depth and complexity. As my skills sharpened through a determination to explore untried rules using silk, I started to cut finer and finer shapes which were then freely embroidered onto a quilted surface. With the aquatic fluidity of a snorkeling scene a la Cousteau (a French personality who also found his calling in America), "Discovery" is the silkollage that displays most vividly the treasures I have found at the core of my creativity, through deeper and deeper dives, out of the porthole of my third-eye.

DISCOVERY, 18" diameter, Francelise
Dawkins, Glen Falls, New York, 1991;
silks; machine appliquéd,
embroidered, and quilted.

ESCAPADE (#158)

Libby Lehman

This quilt is the latest in a series of ribbon quilts. The design for the background was sketched out on graph paper, and the ribbon design was drawn freehand. A studio art quiltmaker by profession, I work on one quilt at a time, from start to finish ("finish" means the slides are taken and labeled); consequently, this quilt took me about three weeks to complete. Having the Museum of the American Quilter's Society add "Escapade" to their collection was a thrill I'm still enjoying!

ESCAPADE, 80" x 80", Libby Lehman,
Houston, Texas, 1992; cotton, rayon and
metallic thread; machine pieced, machine
embroidered, and machine quilted;
First Place Award, Other Techniques,
1993 AQS Show, ©1993.

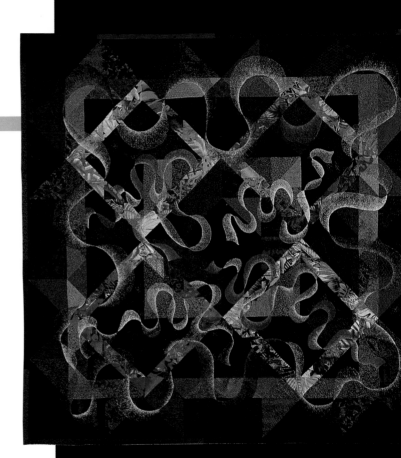

FEAR OF THE DARK (#166)

Since childhood, I had been intrigued by the blips of light and roiling color some of us see when closing our eyes tightly, or when relaxing, waiting for sleep. In 1992 I developed my "spontaneous Log Cabin" method of construction to finally bring my impressions to life. Using a variety of solid black fabrics, some of them cut into tiny strips, I constructed 460 blocks from which I chose 256 for this quilt. Adrift in the floating colors and patterns are a few of the "fears" that crop up at night. On the back is a giant pieced Log Cabin block, a reference to the quilt's traditional parentage.

Mary L. Hackett

FEAR OF THE DARK, 87" x 87",
Mary L. Hackett, Carterville, Illinois,
1993; mostly cottons plus a wide
variety of synthetics – anything black
was not rejected; machine pieced
and machine quilted; Honorable
Mention Award, 1994 AQS Show.

FEATHERED STAR BOUQUET (#119)

Doris Amiss Rabey

In creating this quilt, I started to make a flower appliqué quilt, and as often happens to me, I was not satisfied with the layout and decided to change my whole concept. I made a large Feathered Star center and placed various flower pots around it. I added multiple borders and quilted them heavily. After various setbacks, changes, and running out of one fabric, this quilt was completed in a little over a year. With each quilt, wallhanging, or challenge block I make, I find a new technique to try – in this case it was strip piecing for the center stars. That is what keeps quilting so interesting, so satisfying, and so fulfilling. I've been quilting 18 years now and only wish I had started sooner.

FEATHERED STAR BOUQUET,
77" x 77", Doris Amiss Rabey,
Hyattsville, Maryland, 1987; cottons;
machine pieced, hand appliquéd,
and hand quilted.

FLORAL URNS (#156)

Debra Wagner

I am a traditionalist in design, if not in technique. A machine embroiderer for over twenty years, with a degree in clothing, textiles, and design, my main interest is in developing machine methods for traditional quiltmaking. This quilt was inspired by a set of nineteenth-century quilts. The set and basic motifs were influenced by an 1860 quilt by Mrs. C. Bartlett. The coloration and tone were inspired by two matching quilts attributed to Mary Brown, one made in 1845 and the other in 1852. I was drawn to the general sense of riot and exuberance these quilts displayed.

FLORAL URNS, 90" x 90", Debra Wagner, Cosmos, Minnesota, 1992; cottons; machine pieced, machine appliquéd, machine embroidered, and machine quilted; Bernina Machine Workmanship Award, 1993 AQS Show.

FREEDOM'S CASCADE (#126)

Erika Carter

I have always been interested in needle arts. In 1984, I was doing a lot of knitting when the yarn shop I frequented offered a quilting class. I was immediately hooked. "Freedom's Cascade" was inspired by the dramatic changes which occurred in East Germany with the breaking-up of the Berlin Wall. The gray, black, and white background symbolizes life under communist rule, a presence which greatly impacts the developing democracy represented by the confetti-like flowers.

FREEDOM'S CASCADE, 45" x 68",
Erika Carter, Bellevue, Washington,
1990; cottons; machine pieced,
hand appliquéd, and hand quilted.

GARDEN PARTY (#124)

"Garden Party" was made for two purposes: to hang on my living room wall and incorporate all the colors in my art collection and furnishings, and to be submitted for *Quilter's Newsletter Magazine's* 200th issue, which required the use of a pattern or inspiration from a pattern or quilt in their previous 200 issues. The most challenging aspect of designing the quilt was to place all the animals in a harmonious way so that they would all be looking in the direction of the serpent. Twining the snake on the vine in a realistic manner also took hours of playing with a flexible curve and piece of cording.

Faye Anderson

GARDEN PARTY, 83" x 98", Faye Anderson, Boulder, Colorado, 1987; cottons; machine pieced, hand appliquéd, hand embroidered, and hand quilted.

GENETIC ENGINEERING BRINGS YOU DESIGNER CHRISTMAS TREES (#105)

Adrien Rothschild

This original design quilt is the third in a series featuring this block. I studied molecular biology at John Hopkins as an undergraduate at the time genetic engineering came into being. I wanted to make a design with colorful Christmas trees and thought genetic engineering could explain the colors. These days it's designer jeans, designer this, designer that. Why not Christmas trees color-coordinated with livingroom decor?

GENETIC ENGINEERING BRINGS YOU
DESIGNER CHRISTMAS TREES,
62" x 62", Adrien Rothschild,
Baltimore, Maryland, ©1990; hand-
dyed cottons; hand quilted;
Second Place Award,
Wall Quilt, Amateur, 1991 AQS Show.
PHOTO: AARON M. LEVIN

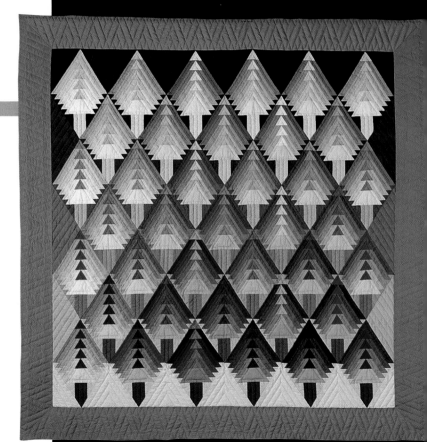

HAMMERED AT HOME (#163)

This quilt has introduced me to a wonderful way to incorporate my immediate environment in my quilts. The images found on this quilt were made by taking leaves from trees, placing them directly on muslin treated with a mordant, and hammering the liquid, which is the dye, out of each leaf. The separate leaf images of kiwi leaves, tulip poplar, ferns, and sweet gum surround the very large juvenile Empress tree leaf. These hand-hammered block designs were arranged to form the design of the quilt, and penwork was added to delineate the veins in the leaves.

Iris Aycock

HAMMERED AT HOME, 78" x 79",
Iris Aycock, Woodville, Alabama, 1994;
cottons; machine pieced and
machine quilted; Best Wall Quilt Award,
1994 AQS Show.

HERE BETWEEN (#147)

Marilyn Henrion

While the quilts I make are all my original designs, they are firmly rooted in the traditional craft of quiltmaking. The works form a bridge between traditional and contemporary avant garde fiber arts. All the pieces are hand quilted and crafted to last. "Here Between" was created for the American Quilt Study Group, and takes its title from a T. S. Eliot poem which seems particularly apt:

Here between the hither and farther shore,
While time is withdrawn, consider the future
And the past with an equal mind...."

HERE BETWEEN, 40" x 40", Marilyn Henrion, New York, New York, 1992; cottons; machine pieced and hand quilted.

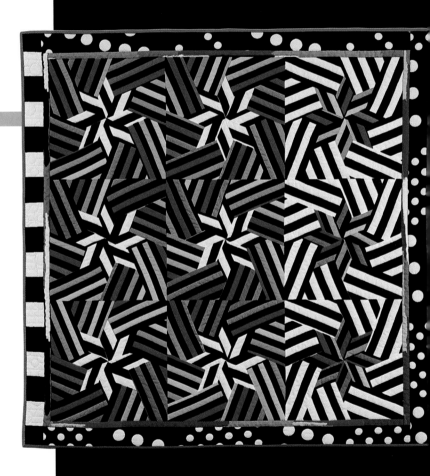

ICE FANTASIA (#137)

Elsie Vredenburg

The inspiration for this quilt was the 1988 Winter Olympics figure skating competition and the 1990 AQS show theme – Fans. I'm not sure just when it occurred to me to combine the two ideas but what finally resulted was a play on the word fan. The people blocks were designed to represent the skater's audience, her fans. In making this quilt I discovered that a slip of the scissors isn't necessarily the end of the world. I cut the center too small in one direction. The solid color strips of the inner border were my solution for getting the people to fit evenly. If you look closely, you'll see there are different lengths on the ends than on the sides. Sometimes a mistake can be the creative nudge I need.

ICE FANTASIA, 74" x 87",
Elsie Vredenburg, Tustin, Michigan,
1989; cottons; machine pieced and
hand quilted; Second Place Award,
Theme (Fans), 1990 AQS Show.

INDIAN SUMMER (#167)

Sherry Sunday

This quilt "Indian Summer" was designed from the autumnal woodlands of Central Pennsylvania and as a remembrance of the bittersweet passage of a daughter from childhood to womanhood. The poem on the back of the quilt was written for this quilt by my eldest daughter, Heather Emily.

INDIAN SUMMER

Silent lightless hours of slumber abruptly awaken
to a barren forest of sterile shimmering trees.

The crisp crackling breath of autumn
cuts deep through the last slice of sun
offered down graciously by Helios,

Tenth-month thankfully accepting,
smiling through frozen tears.

One last bloom of pink splashes up from the garden
and drowns, reincarnated russet
in a cornucopia centerpiece.

Heather Emily Sunday, 1993

INDIAN SUMMER, 106" x 106",
Sherry Sunday, New Kingstown,
Pennsylvania, 1993; cottons; machine
pieced and appliquéd, machine quilted.

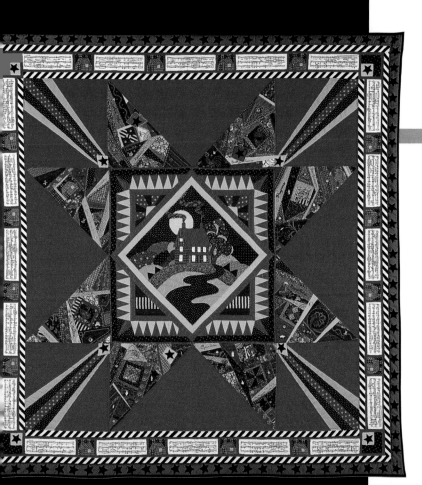

INDIANA CRAZY (#113)

Linda Karel Sage

Coming from a printmaking background, I had most often worked in black & white. Excited by the prospect of working in color, ideas began to develop at an ever-increasing rate. The new ideas seemed to be five years ahead of my ability to actually produce the work, so I tried to develop techniques that would allow me to work faster. In "Indiana Crazy" the crazy-work patches are stitched on a muslin backing in the traditional quilt method – like Log Cabin blocks. They were embellished and pieced into the overall quilt design, and then layered with batting and backing. The piece is hand quilted, but the crazy-patches are tied from front to back – thus saving me considerable time in both assembly and quilting. An Inko-Dye photo of my mother, Jeanette Karel Sage, who taught me to sew, is included among the patches as a tribute and a remembrance.

INDIANA CRAZY, 70" x 70", Linda Karel Sage,
Morgantown, Indiana, 1988; cottons and blends
(some hand dyed and painted); machine and
hand pieced, hand appliquéd, embroidered,
and hand quilted.

JAVANESE JUNGLE (#123)

Audree L. Sells

This quilt was my first attempt at pictorial appliqué. I began quilting in 1986 with very little knowledge of what was going on in the contemporary quilt world. The design for this quilt was adapted from an original batik by Emilie VonKerchoff, a Dutch artist known for her paintings and batiks. It was featured on the cover of *Needlecraft: The Home Arts Magazine*, in November 1933.

JAVANESE JUNGLE, 75" x 94",
Audree L. Sells, Chaska, Minnesota,
1987; cottons; hand appliquéd, hand
embroidered, hand quilted and
beaded; First Place Award,
Appliqué, Amateur, 1988 AQS Show.

JUST FANTASTIC (#136)

"Just Fantastic" is an original design for which I dyed and screen printed all the fabrics, using a secondary triad color scheme. Each hexagon represents two fans. Since I do lap quilting, the whole quilt was not put together before quilting began. In fact, I wasn't sure what I wanted to do for a border until the center portion was quilted and put together. It was a case of good luck – the finished product is one that pleases me. Quiltmaking is a full-time occupation for me because I enjoy it so much. My favorite part is the design process.

Hallie H. O'Kelley

JUST FANTASTIC, 70" x 93", Hallie H. O'Kelley, Tuscaloosa, Alabama, 1990; cottons; machine pieced and hand quilted; Honorable Mention Award, 1990 AQS Show; on permanent loan.

LILIES OF AUTUMN (#152)

Juanita Gibson-Yeager

I work with needle and thread, cloth and beads, and consider myself a quiltmaker. My work salutes nature and celebrates all the beauty in the universe that I can see or imagine. My work echoes the colors of the seasons, too, and sings of the joy I find in seeing leaves flutter and flowers bloom, or seeing birds on extended wings soaring with butterflies in the wind. I came to quiltmaking with no art training, only a desire and strong emotional commitment to create visual beauty with my hands from cloth.

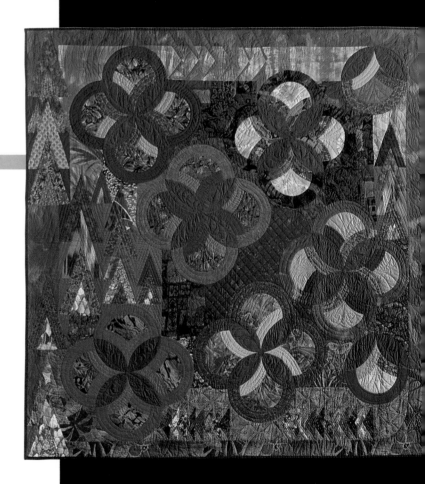

LILIES OF AUTUMN, 70" x 74", Juanita Gibson-Yeager, Louisville, Kentucky, 1991; cottons; machine pieced and hand quilted.

MOMMA'S GARDEN (#140)

Anne Oliver

Since I am a procrastinator and have already completed quilts for my whole family, my incentive to keep on quilting comes from competitive shows. They require discipline and professionalism in my work, but also allow me to express my personality through my quilts. The design for "Momma's Garden" came from a 100-year-old Mennonite counterpane, though the ornate design was modified and appliqué was added for highlights. I use freezer paper for everything. If I can't design by folding or tracing with freezer paper, I won't make the quilt. It took three years to finally decide to tackle this project, but once I began, I completed the quilt in eight months.

MOMMA'S GARDEN, 88" x 91",
Anne Oliver, Alexandria, Virginia,
1992; cottons; hand quilted;
Best of Show Award,
1992 AQS Show.

MORNING GLORY (#128)

Mary Chartier

The central circular design for "Morning Glory" came from "Techny Chimes," a Nancy Pearson pattern that I admired. I stenciled the appliquéd flowers to give them a three-dimensional look. The quilting in the borders presented specific challenges. After I marked the longest border, I washed it out, wanting something more unusual. That day a quilt magazine arrived featuring a design which fit my quilt border perfectly! This quilt was a pure joy to work on.

MORNING GLORY, 80" x 100",
Mary Chartier, New London, Connecticut,
1986; cottons; hand appliquéd,
hand and machine pieced;
Second Place Award, Appliqué,
Professional, 1988 AQS Show.

MOUNT PLEASANT MINERS (#154)

Nancy S. Brown

My mother taught me to quilt about ten years ago after she took a class. I like the idea of creating something that might last a long, long time. I also like the fact that I could create a large design without requiring a lot of space. I have done some watercolor painting and some drawing but nothing is as satisfying as quiltmaking. This quilt is a tribute to my great-grandfather William Brown, who worked at the Mount Pleasant Mine in Grizzly Flats, California, for 17 years as a blacksmith and later as a superintendent. The design was inspired by an 1870's photo of 36 miners, including my great-grandfather.

MOUNT PLEASANT MINERS,
48" x 55", Nancy S. Brown,
Oakland, California, 1993; cottons;
hand appliquéd, hand quilted,
hand painted, and machine pieced;
Best Wall Quilt Award,
1993 AQS Show.

MOUNT ST. HELENS, DID YOU TREMBLE? (#104)

Joyce B. Peaden

This is a personal poem quilt, the form of which was conceived simultaneously with the poem of the same title, May 25, 1980, the day of the secondary eruption of Mount St. Helens. Paper drawings were made in 1984; and the quilt was made between May 1990 and March 1991.

MOUNT ST. HELENS,
DID YOU TREMBLE?,
79" x 94", Joyce B. Peaden,
Prosser, Washington, 1991; cottons;
hand appliquéd, machine pieced,
Seminole piecing (background),
and hand quilted.

NIGHT BEACONS III (#143)

Vicki L. Johnson

While living in Mendocino, I became very fond of the night skies. When we moved to Soquel, we passed Pigeon Point Lighthouse on each trip between Half Moon Bay and Santa Cruz, a welcoming and spectacular sight. The star in the beam of light is my fractured version of the Evening Star block. The ocean, planets, and moon are painted with fabric paints by me, and soft-edge machine appliqué was used to create the buildings. Eleven stars are pieced into a background of eight-pointed stars made from right triangles. The bottom pieced border is a pattern called Big Dipper – very appropriate for this quilt of stars.

NIGHT BEACON III, 48" x 70", Vicki L. Johnson, Soquel, California, ©1992; cottons, including hand-painted and hand-marbled fabrics; machine pieced, hand appliquéd, soft-edge machine appliquéd, painted, hand and machine quilted.

NIGHT FLOWERS (#145)

Deborah Lynn Ward

"Though a quilter fewer than five years, Debbie had created an impressive body of work considering she was the mother of young children. She had developed machine appliqué and machine quilting techniques and won local competitions at least three of those five years. Her death in 1991 was untimely in every possible way. This piece represents her signature style from which she had gained significant recognition."

– Moneca Calvert
January 1992

NIGHT FLOWERS, Deborah Lynn Ward (1952 – 1991), 57" x 55", Arroyo Grande, California, 1991; cottons; machine pieced and machine quilted.

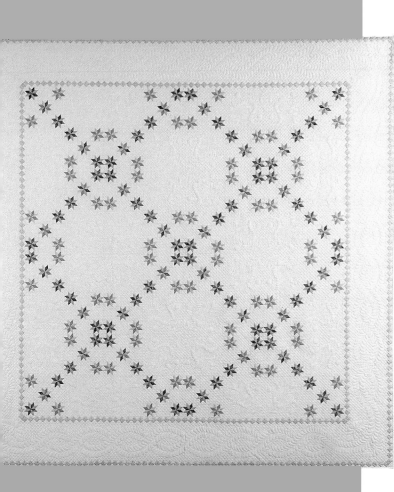

OH, MY STARS (#120)

I decided to make a quilted coverlet when I needed a new bedspread for a high four-poster bed. That coverlet was completed in 1972. Now, I can't imagine not having quilts in the making. The inspiration for "Oh, My Stars" was an antique quilt pictured in *America's Glorious Quilts*. First, I changed the scrap stars to ones with a more controlled color scheme. Then, when I was ready to sew the blocks together, I felt the quilt was not balanced, so I re-arranged the blocks until a very different quilt emerged. Even though someone else's quilt was the inspiration, "Oh, My Stars" turned out to be my own quilt.

Margie T. Karavitis

OH, MY STARS, 97" x 97", Margie T. Karavitis, Spokane, Washington, 1989; cottons; hand pieced and hand quilted; First Place Award, Traditional Pieced, Professional, 1990 AQS Show.

OLDE ENGLISH MEDALLION (#146)

Cindy Vermillion-Davis

In making "Olde English Medallion," inspired by the photo of a quilt with similar design, I attempted to duplicate the colors popular in the mid 1900's. I wanted it to feel like an antique. I have made a series of medallions with important circular centers. I find I am drawn to this format. This quilt has great personal meaning for me. I started it before a very sad and traumatic time in my life, and finished it while working through the pain of divorce. The stitching helped me through one of life's tragedies. I remarried in June 1994 and my new name is Cindy Vermillion Hamilton.

OLDE ENGLISH MEDALLION,
104" x 104", Cindy Vermillion-Davis,
Pagosa Springs, Colorado, 1992;
cottons; hand pieced, hand
appliquéd, and hand quilted;
First Place Award, Traditional Pieced,
1992 AQS Show;
on permanent loan.

ONE FISH, TWO FISH, RED FISH, BLUE FISH (#165)

Using only one fish design, I stretched and squeezed it to create a variety of sizes and shapes. The design is quilted with many different metallic threads. Each fish has different quilting – some have unusual eyes, some have large or small scales, some have overall patterns of stripes or waves. The fish and water fabrics were collected for a long time then combined with a great variety of other fabrics, some hand dyed and painted.

Laura Heine

ONE FISH, TWO FISH, RED FISH,
BLUE FISH, 83" x 91",
Laura Heine, Billings, Montana,
1993; cottons; machine pieced
and machine quilted;
Bernina Workmanship Award,
1994 AQS Show.

OUR SECRET GARDEN (#101)

Donna McConnell

Patricia Eaton

This quilt was a collaboration. I had become ill and needed to rest. One night while watching television, a quilt flashed through my head – a Log Cabin with vines. I knew Donna would be the person to create the Log Cabin, and the vines would be just the project I needed to get back to my quiltmaking. When the quilt had been completed, we decided to name it after Donna's favorite childhood book, *The Secret Garden* by Frances Hodgson Burnett. It seemed appropriate as the quilt had helped me to recover and Donna's friendship is important to each of my days.

– Patricia Eaton
1991

OUR SECRET GARDEN, 87" x 87",
Donna McConnell, Searcy, Arkansas,
and Patricia Eaton, McRae, Arkansas,
1990; cottons; machine pieced
and hand appliquéd.

PANDAS 'ROUND THE WORLD (#168)

Shirley P. Kelly

The center panel of this quilt was inspired by a small reproduction of a poster created by Tom Taylor for Chicago's Field Museum of National History. Membership in the World Wildlife Fund and National Wildlife Federation made me aware of the problems facing the preservation of these shy, elusive animals. At last count, fewer than 1,000 wild pandas – living free – are found in two small preserves in China where human encroachment still threatens what is left of their fragile environment. The figures on the quilt represent one tenth of these pandas. The incredible difficulty of breeding them in captivity does not provide much hope for the continuation of this marvelous animal.

PANDAS 'ROUND THE WORLD,
81" x 106", Shirley P. Kelly,
Colden, New York, 1993; cottons;
hand appliquéd, machine pieced,
and machine quilted; Second Place
Award, Appliqué, Amateur,
1994 AQS Show.

POPPIES AND OTHER CALIFORNIA BEAUTIES (#148)

Canyon Quilters
of San Diego

Canyon Quilters of San Diego is a non-profit group established in 1985 by area women who wished to meet and share their quilting knowledge and skills. This quilt was an opportunity quilt designed by Donalene Rasmussen. Thirty women from the guild appliquéd, pieced, and embroidered the top. Guild members did the quilting. The quilt was a financial and creative success. It raised thousands of dollars for the guild and provided a great sense of satisfaction for those who participated.

POPPIES AND OTHER
CALIFORNIA BEAUTIES, 88" x 112",
Canyon Quilters of San Diego,
San Diego, California, 1990; cottons;
hand appliquéd, hand embroidered,
and hand quilted; Third Place Award,
Group/Team, 1992 AQS Show.

PROGRESSIVE PICTORIAL QUILT (#97)

The making of this quilt was organized by Caron L. Mosey, author of *America's Pictorial Quilts* (AQS, 1985). Caron asked various quiltmakers whose work appeared in her book to contribute their work to a progressive quilt. Each quilter added shapes, working with what was suggested by the pieces already in place on the quilt. Often the next quilter interpreted those shapes in a different way, moving the design in a different direction. The result of this activity was an interesting project and an interesting quilt.

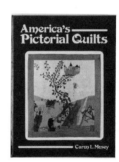

PROGRESSIVE PICTORIAL QUILT,
artists from *America's Pictorial Quilts*,
44" x 44", 1986; cottons.

Contributors to the quilt included Carolyn Muller, Lois K. Ide, Helen Kelley, Pat Cox, Barbara Crane, Paula Nadelstern, Dawn Rappold, Rhoda Cohen, Victoria Faoro, Susan Turbak, Lee Farrington, Jean Johnson, Masami Kato, Linda Cantrell, Elly Dyson, Art Salemme, Erma Martin Yost, Carole Adams, Carole McMichael, Marge Harris, Anita Murphy, Alice Schmude, Jane Miller, Moneca Calvert, Virginia Costa, Joan Schulze, Judy Mathieson, Roberta Horton, Chris Wolf Edmonds, Elaine Sparlin, Ronnie Durrance, Mona Barker, Cathy Grafton, Ed Larson (with Sarah Hass), Steve Schutt, Donna Maki, Gwen Marston, Joe Cunningham, Shannie Coyne. Quilting was done by Caron L. Mosey.

REFLECTION #3 (#98)

Caryl Bryer Fallert

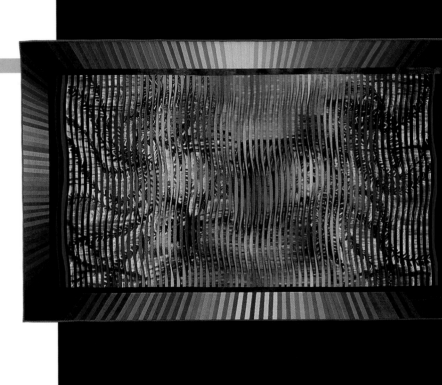

This is one of a series of quilts in which three-dimensional, constructed tucks are pieced onto a patterned background. The background fabric was painted with fiber reactive dyes, and it portrays a memory of Carnarvon Gorge National Park, a beautiful, peaceful place I visited in Australia in 1989. This dramatic gorge is filled with exotic vegetation, some of it prehistoric and found in very few places on earth. In a number of locations throughout the gorge are found 10,000 year old Aboriginal rock paintings in the red and yellow ocher colors of the soil. After a long, hot day of hiking, I climbed into a side canyon called the "Moss Garden," and found a cool, green, peaceful place where both the spirit and the body could rest. This quilt is about the experience of being in that place. The patterns in the background fabric represent the foliage, rocks, streams, and waterfalls of the gorge.

REFLECTION #3, 77" x 45", Caryl Bryer Fallert, Oswego, Illinois, 1990; cottons; machine pieced, hand dyed, hand painted, and machine quilted.

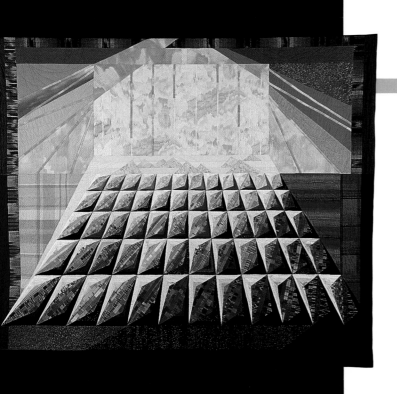

Restoring the Balance (#134)

My family and I have moved many times since I started quilting, but my creative roots are in the mountains and deserts of the Southwest. Nature, and our relationship to the environment have always been important inspirations for my work; I concentrate on the use of color and design to create quilts which are visually exciting and challenging. This quilt was inspired by a hiking trip in the mountains and deserts of Colorado and northern New Mexico. I tried to translate into fabric the feelings I experienced when after hiking for several hours, I came across an incredibly beautiful landscape of wildflowers, rock, and mesas; it was a feeling of joy and elation, mixed with concern that this beauty might not survive for future generations.

Alison Goss

RESTORING THE BALANCE,
95" x 80", Alison Goss, Hockessin,
Delaware, 1990; cottons and
poly-cotton blends; machine pieced
and machine quilted.

RIBBONS & ROSES (#133)

Marie Sturmer

My formal art training began at the Cranbrook Art Academy, and I earned a secondary teaching degree in art education from Alma College and an M.F.A. degree from Wayne University. Years of classroom activities with art students reinforced my ability to adapt many artistic skills and techniques. The stencil-painted quilts of the 1820's fascinate me and have dominated my quilting ventures. The stencil quilt is in a class of its own, special and different from the conventional pieced or patchwork quilt. Today's stencil quilts reflect the grandeur of a bygone era. I take great pride in extending this 170-year-old American style of quiltmaking to the 1990's through my own quilts.

RIBBONS & ROSES, 72" x 86",
Marie Sturmer, Traverse, Michigan,
1989; cottons; stenciled, hand
embroidered, and hand quilted.

RISING MOONS (#121)

Quilting is a wonderful way of expressing yourself and allowing your creative spirit to come forward. Although I have not been trained as an artist, I view my quilts as works of art rather than geometric pieces. This quilt is completely pieced, using twenty-five or more separate templates, all of which fit in a rectangle. I maintain some control, but add separate pieces, such as moons, and fit them into the controlled design. My work has evolved from traditional to contemporary style because I do not like the repetition of blocks. I enjoy it when each piece is a decision. That makes the work slow, but satisfying.

Elaine Stonebraker

RISING MOONS, 72" x 66", Elaine Stonebraker, Scottsdale, Arizona, 1989; cotton; hand pieced, machine and hand quilted; Second Place Award, Pictorial Wall Quilt, 1989 AQS Show.

ROCOCO ISLANDS (#159)

Mary Jo Dalrymple

I used an original design for eight of the blocks in this quilt and the traditional Mariner's Compass for the center block and along the borders. There were four things which I felt were unusual at the time the quilt was made; the original block design, the use of partial compasses, the use of sashing areas to create the look of a medallion style, and the experimentation with large patterned cloth and the use of the fish batik fabric. In "Rococo Islands," I tried to capture the feeling of ocean, sea birds, islands, and sand bars. This was my 12th quilt and I have just finished my 84th.

ROCOCO ISLANDS, 94" x 94", Mary Jo Dalrymple, Omaha, Nebraska, 1982; cottons; hand pieced and hand quilted.

SILVERSWORD – DEGENER'S DREAM (#134)

Louise Young

I have a master's degree in botany, specializing in ecology, so nature and especially plants are very important in my life. Most of my quilts are based on images from the plant world. The silversword plant is endemic to the lava fields of the Hawaiian Islands, and it is listed on the international endangered species list. The title of this quilt also honors Otto Degener, a botanist who has worked to catalog and preserve the native flora of Hawaii. In this, my first Hawaiian quilt, I tried to follow all of the quiltmaking traditions from Hawaii. This quilt has changed my outlook on quilting – I no longer feel I have to do anything in precise, straight lines.

SILVERSWORD – DEGENER'S DREAM,
97" x 97", Louise Young, Tioga,
Pennsylvania, ©1988; cotton;
hand appliquéd and hand quilted;
First Place Award, Appliqué, Amateur,
1989 AQS Show.

SOPHISTICATION (#161)

Margaret M. Rudd

The design for this quilt was developed by Ross Tucker, a student at Corydon Middle School in Corydon, Indiana. The quilt was made in conjunction with a special project at the middle school which resulted in a book of contemporary designs created with "the vision of youth and the skill of maturity." The project grew out of a comment I made when I saw the work students in this school were creating in art classes taught by my daughter, Rudee Rodrîguez. The quality of their work led me to comment, "The students' designs should be published." The result was *Capitalizing Designs*, a book featuring students' designs and photos of quilts executed in those designs by experienced quilters.

SOPHISTICATION, 55" x 55",
Margaret M. Rudd, Cadiz, Kentucky,
1987; cotton, silk, suede cloth;
machine pieced and hand quilted.

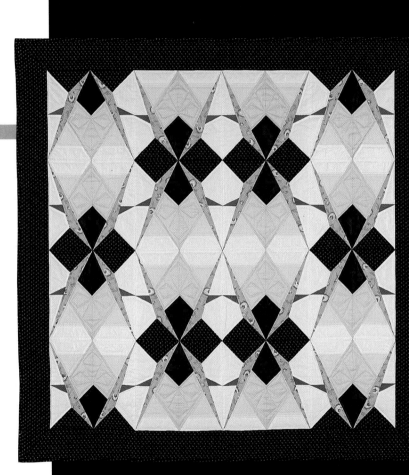

SQUARE WITHIN A SQUARE WITHIN A SQUARE (#117)

Various forms of art have always been a source of pleasure to me. Painting, sculpture, and jewelry making led me to the new art of making quilts. My quilting experience really began around 1983, while I was working in a quilt shop. Although I have a B.S. in art and interior decoration, I have a tremendous amount to learn in the areas of quilt construction techniques. Using fabrics instead of paint, and scissors instead of drawing have involved great pleasure and revelation.

Ruth Britton Smalley

SQUARE WITHIN A SQUARE
WITHIN A SQUARE, 100" x 99",
Ruth Britton Smalley, Houston, Texas,
1986; cottons; machine pieced and
hand quilted; Third Place Award,
Theme (Log Cabin), 1987 AQS Show.

STARBURST (#154)

Judy Sogn

This Feathered Star quilt remains my favorite quilt so far. I enjoy using small multicolored prints which appear as solids from a distance. When viewed close-up they give added texture and interest to the quilt. For the American Quilter's Society Show and Contest, I entered "Starburst" in the traditional category rather than the theme category of Stars, because I felt it represented my love of traditional patterns. This quilt is a variation of my quilt "Forever Green," which was inspired by Margit Echols' block called Stars and Pines.

STARBURST, 94" x 94", Judy Sogn,
Seattle, Washington, 1990; cottons;
machine pieced and hand quilted;
Second Place Award,
Traditional Pieced, Professional,
1991 AQS Show.

STELLA ANTIGUA (#155)

Hanne Vibeke
De Koning-Stapel

This quilt is a memory of a sailing trip in the Caribbean. Our youngest son sailed the Atlantic Ocean and we joined him in Antigua. On this trip I started piecing the Lone Star part. It was meant as an octagonal tablecloth, but my husband didn't like it on the table. So it went into the cupboard. After some months I thought out how to make a bed quilt out of it, and it lay on the bed in our guest room for some time and was a nice memory of our sailing trip. Since April 1993 it has been in the MAQS Collection.

STELLA ANTIGUA, 91" x 91", Hanne Vibeke de Koning-Stapel, Bilthoven, Holland, 1988; silks; hand pieced, hand appliquéd, and hand quilted; First Place Award, Traditional Pieced, Professional, 1989 AQS Show.

SUBMERGENCE (#127)

Erika Carter

"Submergence" is one of my water quilts, suggesting through color the attractiveness of the ocean, the desire to explore its mysteries. Though the water's surface seems just within hand's reach, the depths hold our attention. However, not being a swimmer, I've experienced being caught underwater and needing to be fished out. The water's surface was bright with sunlight, but to me, unattainable. Yet when I look at this quilt I can imagine being surrounded by water and unafraid. This is the third in a series of water quilts.

SUBMERGENCE, 53" x 71",
Erika Carter, Bellevue, Washington,
1989; cottons; machine pieced
and hand quilted.

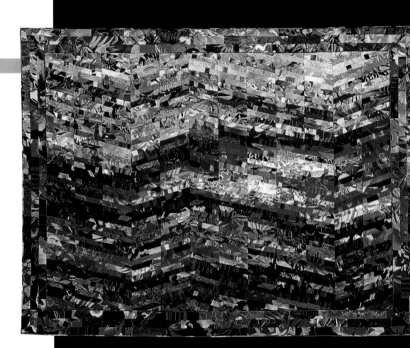

TENNESSEE PINK MARBLE (#103)

The first quilt I entered in competition won a blue ribbon and that spurred me on. Now I use shows as a learning experience. It's impossible for me to evaluate my work until I see it compared to other quilts. "Tennessee Pink Marble" is based on the Spring Blossom pattern. A marbleized fabric of pink and green was used as an outer border, hence the name, because it resembles the pink marble of Tennessee. As quilting is only a hobby for me, I never sell my quilts. I still have them all, with the exception of this one.

Julia Overton
Needham

TENNESSEE PINK MARBLE,
72" x 88", Julia Overton Needham,
Knoxville, Tennessee, 1990; cottons
and cotton blends; hand pieced,
hand appliquéd, and hand quilted;
Gingher Workmanship Award,
1991 AQS Show.

TOUJOURS NOUVEAU (#157)

Suzanne Marshall

My husband, Garland, loves Art Nouveau designs, so I started searching for ideas for an Art Nouveau quilt. I found a Dover Publication book, *Art Nouveau Designs* by Ed Sibbett, Jr., which contained black and white drawings, four of which especially caught my eye and provided the starting point for the quilt. "Toujours Nouveau" is the most difficult quilt that I have made. The twisted ribbons were especially complex. Manipulating three shades of fabric that were continuously intertwining, showing first the front and then the back side of the ribbons, was exceptionally challenging.

TOUJOURS NOUVEAU, 68" x 80",
Suzanne Marshall, Clayton, Missouri,
1993; cottons; hand appliquéd, hand
embroidered, and hand quilted;
Gingher Award for Hand Workmanship,
1993 AQS Show.

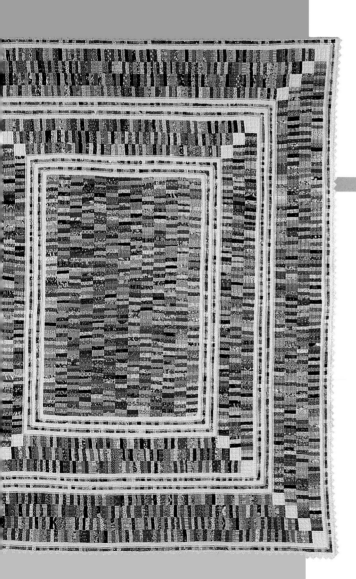

WASTE NOT, WANT NOT (#122)

Each year I attend a three-day seminar with approximately 50 women in attendance which is sponsored by our Poulsbo, Washington, Quilt Group of 136 members. A large sack labeled "Louise's Scrap Collection" is conveniently placed for all to toss in their small clippings of materials from the project they are working on at the time – hence the rainbow of colors in this quilt. This quilt has 5,976 print pieces of 1½" and 2½" strips of various widths in many bright colors. One-inch muslin strips edged with ¼" lace create the rectangles. I have two large flat suit boxes under the bed and will add more small pieces sorted by colors, until I have 7,000 to make another quilt.

Louise Stafford

WASTE NOT, WANT NOT, 83" x 96",
Louise Stafford, Bremerton,
Washington, 1990; cottons and
cotton blends; machine pieced and
hand quilted.

WHEN GRANDMOTHER'S LILY GARDEN BLOOMS (#125)

Eileen Bahring Sullivan

Retiring from teaching in 1972 to raise a family and pursue my own art, I became involved in quiltmaking "innocently and very traditionally" in the late 1970's. I began entering juried competitions with the first AQS show in 1985, and have continued. I use quilting as a form of expression for visual images rather than a "functional" craft. I feel strongly about both good design and technical excellence and aim to meet the highest standards in both areas.

WHEN GRANDMOTHER'S LILY
GARDEN BLOOMS, 64" x 82",
Eileen Bahring Sullivan, Columbia,
South Carolina, 1990;
cottons and blends; machine pieced,
hand embroidered, and hand
quilted; First Place Award,
Innovative Pieced, Professional,
1990 AQS Show.

WILD ROSE (#162)

I started quilting in 1983 after learning from my grandmother, and I began making quilts for competitions after my marriage in 1989. The idea for "Wild Rose" came from a photograph of a quilt that was partially destroyed in the Chicago fire of 1871. The basic Whig Rose pattern is used, along with ideas from other quilts that I have seen and made.

Fay Pritts

WILD ROSE, 92" x 92",
Fay Pritts, Mount Pleasant,
Pennsylvania, 1993; cottons;
hand appliquéd and hand quilted;
Best of Show Award,
1994 AQS Show.

*The quilts in this publication are regularly displayed
at the Museum of the American Quilter's Society.*

MUSEUM OF THE AMERICAN QUILTER'S SOCIETY (MAQS)
215 Jefferson Street, Paducah, Kentucky

A dream long held by American Quilter's Society founders Bill and Meredith Schroeder and by quilters worldwide was realized on April 25, 1991, when the Museum of the American Quilter's Society (MAQS, pronounced "Max") opened its doors in Paducah, Kentucky. As is stated in brass lettering over the building's entrance, this non-profit institution is dedicated to "honoring today's quilter," by stimulating and supporting the study, appreciation, and development of quiltmaking throughout the world.

The 30,000 square foot facility includes a central exhibition gallery featuring a selection of quilts by contemporary quiltmakers from the museum's permanent collection, and two additional galleries displaying changing exhibits of antique and contemporary quilts. Lectures, workshops, and other related activities are held in the facility's spacious modern classrooms. A gift and book shop makes available a wide selection of fine crafts and quilt books. The museum is open year-round and is handicapped accessible.

For more information, write: MAQS, P.O. Box 1540, Paducah, KY 42002-1540 or phone: 502-442-8856.

BILL and MEREDITH SCHROEDER

For twenty years Bill and Meredith Schroeder have operated a successful publishing company in Paducah, Kentucky.

In 1984 they became interested in quilting. After attending several quilt shows, they decided they would bring attention to the extraordinary work today's quiltmakers were creating. Out of that idea came the American Quilter's Society, the first annual AQS Quilt Show and Contest in 1985, and the first issue of *American Quilter* magazine.

From the beginning the Schroeders sought to increase the respect the public had for quilts and quiltmakers. They developed a show with substantial monetary awards, published a magazine, and developed a membership program.

Today many books are published in addition to *American Quilter* magazine; the AQS annual quilt show awards now exceed $75,000, and other programs such as the quilt referral program have been developed.

Through AQS activities Bill and Meredith came into contact with many of the top quilters from around the country, and they began to do more than admire quilts and support them through AQS activities, they began to purchase them. Gradually a collection developed. Out of a desire to share that collection grew the concept of a museum dedicated to today's quilts, quiltmakers, and quilting.

In the summer of 1990, ground was broken for the building of such a museum. The Schroeder family supported the design and construction of this two million dollar facility, which opened in April 1991.

MAQS is a separate non-profit organization governed by its own board of directors, but co-founders Bill and Meredith Schroeder continue to serve the museum, providing important resources and expertise.

PHOTO: STEVEN McKINLEY

MUSEUM OF THE AMERICAN QUILTER'S SOCIETY

The Museum of the American Quilter's Society was designed expressly for the display of quilts, and its primary activity is the presentation of quilt exhibits. Selections from the museum's own permanent collection are always on display, along with changing exhibits of antique and contemporary quilts. The museum's spacious galleries allow even very large quilts to be viewed from a distance for overall visual impact and design, and then up close for the stunning details.

Exhibits have included selections from major private collections, pieces borrowed from other institutions, and quilts loaned by individuals. Each quilt is displayed with additional information – artists' statements in the case of contemporary quilts, and known information about maker, fabrics and techniques, and other relevant material in the case of antique quilts. Quilts on loan and from the permanent collection have done much to introduce a wider population to

the extraordinary accomplishments of quilters and encourage all to view quilts as valuable contributions to our national culture.

In 1995 MAQS began circulating exhibits to other museums and cultural centers around the country, bringing the excitement of quilting to new facilities and new audiences. An international New Quilts from an Old Favorite contest held each autumn challenges quilters to make innovative quilts based on a specific traditional pattern. The contest finalists and winners then become an exhibit which travels for 18 months. Other exhibits have been prepared for sharing beyond the MAQS facility.

In addition to quilt exhibits, the museum features a gift shop with fine crafts in all media from around the country. Pottery, jewelry, weaving, hand-made paper, wood carving, and other fine craft works exhibiting the same level of craftsmanship and artistry as the quilts in MAQS exhibits are offered for sale in the shop. A second room contains an extraordinary selection of books related to quilting and textiles.

Over 400 different books are on display for selection, from publishers worldwide.

The museum also houses classrooms used for everything from meetings to workshops on quiltmaking, to special events. In-depth workshops with nationally known quilting figures are held in these spacious modern rooms, with students attending from all over the world. These well-equipped rooms offer a comfortable environment for study, and the museum's exhibits and book store offer students additional resources and inspiration.

The Museum of the American Quilter's Society seeks to honor today's quilters in every way possible, encouraging all to appreciate quilts and those who make them. For more information about current programs write: MAQS, PO Box 1540, Paducah, KY 42002-1540 or call 502-442-8856.

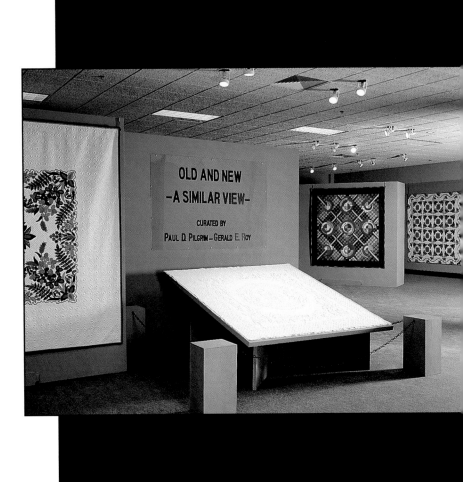

FRIENDS OF MAQS

A non-profit organization, the Museum of the American Quilter's Society is made possible by annual contributions from individuals, businesses, and corporations. Join the Friends of MAQS program, to support MAQS activities and receive information and special opportunities. Friends donating $20 or more receive the Friends of MAQS Newsletter providing information about exhibits and activities, and enjoy free admission to the MAQS galleries. Friends donating $100 or more are recognized in the museum's lobby.

Become a Friend of MAQS and help us honor today's quilter.

MAQS Friend/Gift Donation

To become a Friend of MAQS or give a gift donation complete the coupon and mail with your donation to:
MAQS, P.O. Box 1540, Paducah, KY 42002-1540

Name_____Address_____

City_____State_____Zip_____Telephone_____
I would like to make the following donation:
    ❏ Basic $20 ❏ Associate $50 ❏ Benefactor $100 ❏ Patron $500 ❏ President's Club $1,000

Enclosed is $_____payable to MAQS or charge to my ❏ VISA ❏ Mastercard

Credit Card #_____

Name_____

Signature_____
    ❏ Gift Contribution ❏ Contribution in honor of ❏ Contribution in memory of ❏ Regular Contribution

Name of person in whose name you are giving or to whom you are paying tribute_____

Their address_____City_____State_____Zip_____

Acknowledgement of Tribute to be sent to_____

Their address_____City_____State_____Zip_____

Quilts and Quiltmakers included in
QUILTS: THE PERMANENT COLLECTION – MAQS, VOL. I

Quilts and Quiltmakers included in
QUILTS: THE PERMANENT COLLECTION – MAQS, VOL. I

Index to Quiltmakers
QUILTS: THE PERMANENT COLLECTION – MAQS, VOL. II

Index to Quilts
QUILTS: THE PERMANENT COLLECTION – MAQS, VOL. II

OTHER MAQS EXHIBIT PUBLICATIONS

These books can be found in the MAQS bookshop and in local bookstores and quilt shops. If you are unable to locate a title in your area, you can order by mail from the publisher: AQS, P.O. Box 3290, Paducah, KY 42002-3290.

Please add $1 for the first book and $.40 for each additional one to cover postage and handling. International orders please add $1.50 for the first book and $1 for each additional one.

To order by VISA or MASTERCARD call: 1-800-626-5420 or fax: 1-502-898-8890.

Nancy Crow: Work in Transition
Nancy Crow
#3331: AQS, 1992, 32 pages, 9" x 10", softbound, $12.95.

New Jersey Quilts – 1777 to 1950: Contributions to an American Tradition
The Heritage Quilt Project of New Jersey
#3332: AQS, 1992, 256 pages, 8½" x 11", softbound, $29.95.

Quilts: Old and New, A Similar View
Paul D. Pilgrim and Gerald E. Roy
#3715: AQS, 1993, 40 pages, 8¾" x 8", softbound, $12.95.

Quilts: The Permanent Collection – MAQS
#2257: AQS, 1991, 100 pages, 10" x 6½", softbound, $9.95.

The Log Cabin Returns to Kentucky: Quilts from the Pilgrim/Roy Collection
Paul D. Pilgrim and Gerald E. Roy
#3329: AQS, 1992, 36 pages, 9" x 7", softbound, $12.95.

Victorian Quilts, 1875-1900: They Aren't All Crazy
Paul D. Pilgrim and Gerald E. Roy
#3932: AQS, 1994, 64 pages, 6" x 9", softbound, $14.95.